Super Simple
Throw & Catch

Healthy & Fun Activities to Move Your Body

Nancy Tuminelly

Contributing Physical Education Consultant, Linn Ahrendt, Power Play Education, Inc.
Consulting Editor, Diane Craig, M.A./Reading Specialist

A Division of ABDO

ABDO
Publishing Company

visit us at www.abdopublishing.com

Published by ABDO Publishing Company, a division of the ABDO Group, P.O. Box 398166, Minneapolis, Minnesota 55439. Copyright © 2012 by Abdo Consulting Group, Inc. International copyrights reserved in all countries. No part of this book may be reproduced in any form without written permission from the publisher. Super SandCastle™ is a trademark and logo of ABDO Publishing Company.

Printed in the United States of America, North Mankato, Minnesota
052011
092011

 PRINTED ON RECYCLED PAPER

Editor: Liz Salzmann
Content Development: Nancy Tuminelly, Linn Ahrendt
Cover and Interior Design and Production: Colleen Dolphin, Mighty Media, Inc.
Photo Credits: Colleen Dolphin, Shutterstock

The following manufacturers/names appearing in this book are trademarks: Target®

Library of Congress Cataloging-in-Publication Data

Tuminelly, Nancy, 1952-
  Super simple throw & catch : healthy & fun activities to move your body / Nancy Tuminelly.
    p. cm. -- (Super simple exercise)
  ISBN 978-1-61714-963-4
  1. Physical fitness for children--Juvenile literature. I. Title.
  GV443.T86 2012
  613.7'042--dc22
                                                            2011000964

Super SandCastle™ books are created by a team of professional educators, reading specialists, and content developers around five essential components—phonemic awareness, phonics, vocabulary, text comprehension, and fluency—to assist young readers as they develop reading skills and strategies and increase their general knowledge. All books are written, reviewed, and leveled for guided reading, early reading intervention, and Accelerated Reader® programs for use in shared, guided, and independent reading and writing activities to support a balanced approach to literacy instruction.

Note to Adults

This book is all about encouraging children to be active and play! Avoid having children compete against each other. At this age, the idea is for them to have fun and learn basic skills. Some of the activities in the book require adult assistance and/or permission. Make sure children play in appropriate spaces free of objects that can cause accidents or injuries. Stay with children at the park, playground, or mall, or when going for a walk. Make sure children wear appropriate shoes and clothing for comfort and ease of movement.

Contents

Time to Throw & Catch!

Being active is one part of being healthy. You should move your body for at least one hour every day! You don't have to do it all at one time. It all adds up.

Being active gives you **energy** and helps your body grow strong. There are super simple ways to move your body. Two of them are throwing and catching. This book has fun and easy activities to get you started. Try them or make up your own.

Do You Know?
Being Active Helps You

1 be more relaxed and less stressed

2 feel better about yourself and what you can do

3 be more ready to learn and do well in school

4 rest better and sleep well at night

5 build strong bones, **muscles**, and joints

So turn off the TV, computer, or phone. Get up and start throwing and catching!

Muscle Mania

You have **muscles** all over your body. You use them whenever you move any part of your body. The more you move your muscles, the stronger they get!

arm

neck

shoulder

stomach

chest

back

upper leg

lower leg

Healthy Eating

You need **energy** to move your body. Good food gives your body energy. Some good foods are fruits, vegetables, milk, lean meat, fish, and bread. Foods such as pizza, hamburgers, French fries, and candy are okay sometimes. But you shouldn't eat them all the time.

Remember!

☑ Eating right every day is as important as being active every day

☑ Eat three healthy meals every day

☑ Eat five **servings** of fruits and vegetables every day

☑ Eat healthy snacks

☑ Eat fewer fast foods

☑ Drink a lot of water

☑ Eat less sugar, salt, and fat

Move It Chart

Make a chart to record how much time you spend doing things. Put your chart where you will see it often. This will help you remember to fill it out every day. See if you move your body at least an hour each day.

Move It Chart
Week of March 8-14

Activity	Sunday	Monday	Tuesday	Wednesday	Thursday	Friday	Saturday
baseball	●		●	●	●		●
Bottle Bowling	●					●	
take out the garbage			●			●	

1 Put the title of your chart at the top of a piece of paper. Then put "Week of" and a line for the dates.

2 Make a chart with eight **columns**. Put "activity" at the top of the first column. Put the days of the week at the top of the other columns. Under "activity," list all of the things you do. Include sports, games, and **chores**. Don't forget the activities in this book! Put "total time" at the bottom. Make copies of the chart.

3 Start a new chart each week. Put the dates at the top.

4 Mark how much time you spend on each activity each day. Be creative! Use different colors, **symbols**, or clock faces. For example, a blue sticker could mean 15 minutes of movement. A purple sticker could mean 60 minutes of movement.

◡ = 10 minutes ⚪ = 30 minutes

🔴 = 15 minutes 🔵 = 60 minutes

5 Add up each day's activity. Did you move your body at least an hour every day?

Tools & Supplies

Here are some of the things you will need to get started.

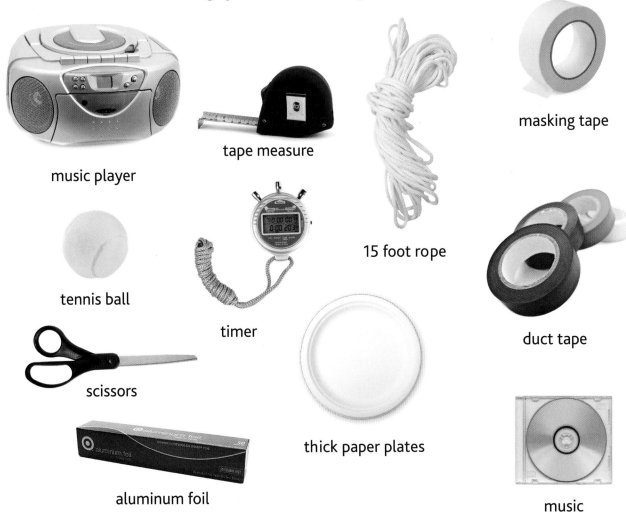

music player

tape measure

15 foot rope

masking tape

tennis ball

timer

duct tape

scissors

thick paper plates

aluminum foil

music

markers

chalk

socks

plastic bowls

clear tape

foam ball

beach ball

paper bag

plastic bottle with cap

softball

plastic cup

rubber ball

Hot Potato

Pretend you have a hot potato! Don't burn your hands!

WHAT YOU NEED

paper
pen or pencil
bowl
tennis ball
music player
music

MUSCLES USED

leg
arm
shoulder
neck

TIME

15-20 minutes

1. Write different exercises on pieces of paper. Use the suggestions below or think of your own!
   - Jump up and down 10 times.
   - Run around the circle five times.
   - Hop on each foot five times.
   - Touch your toes 10 times.
   - Skip around the circle five times.
   - Make 10 big circles with your arms.

2. Fold each paper. Put the pieces of paper in the bowl.

3. Sit in a circle. Put the bowl in the middle. Start the music. Throw the ball around the circle. Pretend the ball is very hot! Throw it quickly.

4. When the song is over the player holding the ball takes a paper out of the box. He or she reads it out loud.

5. That player does what the paper says. Then he or she sits back down. Start a new song. Toss the ball again.

13

Bag Hoops

Play basketball anywhere and anytime!

WHAT YOU NEED

paper bag
scissors
duct tape
rubber ball
chalk
tape measure

MUSCLES USED

leg
arm
shoulder

TIME

10-20 minutes

14

1. Cut the bottom out of the paper bag. Have an adult tape the bag to a wall or **garage** door. The top should be about 6 feet (2 m) from the ground. This is the basket!

2. Use **chalk** or tape to mark six spots around the basket to throw from. Make two close marks, two on each side, and two farther away.

3. Stand on one of the spots. Aim for the basket and throw. Keep trying until you make a basket from that spot. Then stand on a different spot.

4. Try running up to the basket and throwing the ball. Keep trying to run and make baskets from different spots.

➡ The bag might rip, so have some extras **handy**!

Flying Saucer

Make your own disk to throw and catch!

WHAT YOU NEED

thick paper plate
markers
large sheet of paper
tape

MUSCLES USED

leg
arm
shoulder
back
stomach

TIME

15-30 minutes

16

1. Have fun decorating the plate with markers.

2. Get some friends together. Throw the flying saucer to each other.

3. Draw a bull's-eye on a large sheet of paper.

4. Tape the bull's-eye to a tree. Try to hit the middle of the bull's-eye with the flying saucer.

5. How long can you run around throwing and catching the flying saucer? Play for 15 minutes. Take a break. Then try to play for 30 minutes.

Sock Toss

Have you ever used a pair of rolled-up socks as a ball?

WHAT YOU NEED

clear tape
6 bowls, different sizes
paper
markers
6 pairs of socks, rolled
notebook

MUSCLES USED

arm
shoulder

TIME

10-15 minutes

1. Use tape to mark a throw line on the ground. Put the bowls on one side of the throw line. They should be different **distances** from the line.

2. Make points signs with paper and markers. Tape a sign to each bowl.
   - 1 point for large bowls close to the throw line.
   - 2 points for **medium** bowls.
   - 3 or 4 points for small bowls far away from the throw line.

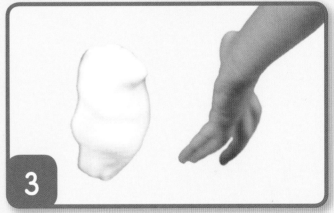

3. Stand behind the line. Throw the rolled socks into the bowls. Each player throws three pairs of socks per turn.

4. Record the points for each bowl a pair of socks lands in. Add up the points and try again!

19

Beach Ball Bop

You better keep your eyes on the ball!

WHAT YOU NEED

music player
music
beach ball

MUSCLES USED

leg
arm
shoulder
neck

TIME

15-30 minutes

1. Start the music. Throw the ball in the air and catch it. Keep throwing and catching it until the song is over.

2. Start the music again. Throw the ball up, but don't catch it. Instead, hit it back up in the air with your hands. Count how many times you can do it. Stop when the song is over.

3. Start the music again. Throw the ball up. This time use other body parts to keep the ball in the air. Try your knees, head, fists, elbows, feet, or back. Stop when the song is over. Sit down and rest.

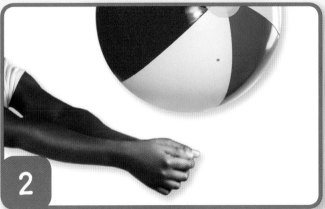

Bottle Bowling

Score a strike with this fun game!

WHAT YOU NEED

10 plastic bottles with caps
masking tape
tape measure
softball
paper
pen

MUSCLES USED

leg
arm
shoulder

TIME

15-30 minutes

1. Put about 2 inches (5 cm) of water in each bottle. Screw the caps on tightly.

2. Put the bottles in a triangle. Make a tape triangle on the ground around the bottles.

3. Put a line of tape 10 feet (3 m) away from the front bottle.

4. Stand three steps behind the line with the ball in one hand. Take three steps forward. Swing your arm back, bend down, and roll the ball toward the bottles. Do not step over the line.

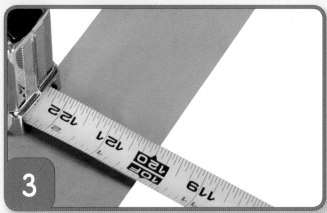

5. Each player takes three turns. Write down how many bottles each player knocks over. See who can knock them all over!

Ball in the Bag

A great way to practice throwing and catching!

WHAT YOU NEED

rope or clothesline
tape measure
2 paper bags or buckets
timer
4 foam balls for
   each player

MUSCLES USED

leg
arm
shoulder

TIME

15-30 minutes

1. Tie the rope about 5 feet (1.5 m) high between two trees or posts.

2. **Divide** into two teams. Each team stands on one side of the rope. Put a paper bag on each side. Each bag should have four balls for each player.

3. Someone says "Go!" Each player throws a ball from their team's bag over the rope.

4. A player who catches a ball puts it in their bag. Then the player takes a ball out and throws it. The players keep taking balls out and putting balls in the bag.

5. After 10 minutes, someone says Stop! See which team has the most balls in their bag.

Cup Catch

Who needs a ball and glove to play catch?

WHAT YOU NEED

plastic cups
aluminum foil

MUSCLES USED

leg
arm
shoulder
back
neck

TIME

5-10 minutes

1. Roll up some **aluminum foil** to make a ball. The ball should fit inside the cups. Give each player a cup.

2. One player throws the ball. The second player catches the ball with his or her cup.

3. Then the catcher throws the ball back to the first player. Now the first player tries to catch it. Keep throwing the ball back and forth.

4. Move farther away from each other. Try running while throwing and catching.

Two-Square

Easier than Four-Square and just as fun!

WHAT YOU NEED

chalk
tape measure
tennis ball

MUSCLES USED

leg
arm
shoulder
back
stomach

TIME

15-30 minutes

1. Draw an area 10 feet (3 m) long and 5 feet (1.5 m) wide. Draw a line across the center to make two squares.

2. Each player stands in a square. One player **bounces** the tennis ball and hits it to the other player. Use your **palm** like a paddle.

3. The ball must bounce once in the other player's square. Then that player can hit it back. Keep hitting the ball back and forth. See how many times you can do it!

4. If the ball lands outside the squares, start over. Also start over if the ball bounces more than once.

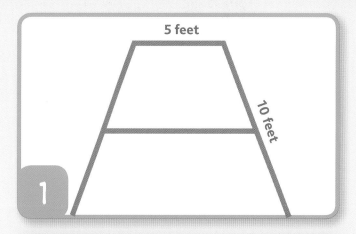

29

Just Keep Moving!

Try these during TV and homework breaks, after meals, or anytime.

Monkey in the Middle

Make sure you have an open space. Use a clean pair of rolled-up socks. One person is in the middle. Two other players throw the socks back and forth over the middle player. If the middle person catches the socks, the person who threw them goes to the middle.

Bean Bag Bash

Throw a bean bag up, turn around and catch it. Throw it up, clap your hands and catch it. Throw it and clap two times. Throw it and clap three times. Now throw a bean bag up from under your right leg, clap, and catch. Do the same under your left leg.

Living Room Basketball

Use rolled-up socks, a soft ball, or **aluminum foil** rolled into a ball. Put a basket or a bucket next to a wall. Throw the ball into the basket. Stand different **distances** away from the basket. Move farther away to make it harder.

Being active is for everyone!

- Ask your family to join in activities at home.
- Have relay races with your classmates at recess.
- Have an adult take you to a safe park to play tag with friends.

Super Simple Moves
Pledge

I promise to be active and move my body for one hour a day, five days a week.
I know that eating right and getting enough sleep are also important.
I want to be healthy and have a strong body.

I will:

- ☑ keep track of my activities on a Move It Chart or something like it

- ☑ ask my friends to stay active with me and set up play times outside three days a week

- ☑ ask my family to plan a physical activity one day a week

- ☑ limit my time watching TV and using the computer, except for homework

- ☑ get up and move my body during TV commercials and homework breaks

To print a pledge certificate, go to www.abdopublishing.com.
For more information about being active, please visit www.letsmove.gov.

31

Glossary

aluminum foil – a thin sheet made of aluminum, which is a light metal.

bounce – to spring up or back after hitting something.

chalk – a stick made of soft rock used to write on blackboards and sidewalks.

chore – a regular job or task, such as cleaning your room.

column – one of the vertical rows in a table or chart.

distance – the amount of space between two places.

divide – to separate into equal groups or parts.

energy – the ability to move, work, or play hard without getting tired.

garage – a room or building that cars are kept in.

handy – close by or easy to get.

medium – not the biggest or the smallest.

muscle – the tissue connected to the bones that allows body parts to move.

palm – the inside of your hand between your wrist and fingers.

serving – a single portion of food.

symbol – an object or picture that stands for or represents something.